Julius Caesar
★
Cleopatra

**BIOGRAPHIES OF
TWO LEADERS FROM
ANCIENT CIVILIZATIONS**

by Sarah Albee

Table of Contents

Focus on the Genre: Biography 2
Tools for Readers and Writers 4
The World and Lives of Julius Caesar and Cleopatra 5
Julius Caesar 8
Cleopatra 18
The Writer's Craft: Biography 30
Glossary 32
Make Connections Across Texts . . . . Inside Back Cover

Focus on the Genre

BIOGRAPHY

What is a biography?

A biography is a factual retelling of another person's life. The person may have lived long ago or in recent history, or the person may still be alive today. Biographies can cover a person's entire life, or just important parts of a person's life. When possible, a biography includes direct quotes from the person. This helps the reader make a connection to the person.

What is the purpose of a biography?

A biography helps a reader understand the people, places, times, and events that were or are important in the subject's life. It provides a summary of the person's major life experiences and achievements. In addition, the way the author writes the biography helps a reader get a sense of the person as a real human being who had (and perhaps still has) an impact on the lives of others.

How do you read a biography?

The title will tell you the subject of the biography and may include something interesting about him or her. The first paragraph will try to "hook" the reader by capturing his or her attention. As you read, note the setting. The setting often influences what happens in a person's life. Also pay close attention to the sequence of events in the person's life. Ask yourself: *Did this event happen to the person, or did the person make it happen? How did this event affect the person's life? What do I admire about this person? Is there something in this person's experiences that I could apply to my life?*

Features of a Biography

- A biography tells the person's date and place of birth.
- A biography starts with a strong "hook."
- A biography tells about the person's family, childhood, and important events.
- A biography describes the person's impact on the world.
- A biography describes the person's personality and characteristics.
- A biography quotes the person and/or people who knew the person.

Who writes biographies?

People who write biographies want to learn more about others' life stories and how those people made their marks on the world. Some people write biographies because they are interested in a certain topic, such as sports, history, or cooking. Others write biographies simply because they are interested in people!

Tools for Readers and Writers

Strong Lead

Writers of biographies try to "hook" readers, or grab their attention, with the first few sentences, or lead. A strong lead tells readers something important about the subject of the biography and hints at why he or she is worth reading about. Writers use two types of leads.
- **direct lead**—tells who or what the piece is about and why the subject is important
- **indirect lead**—may quote someone, ask a question, describe a setting, or tell an anecdote, or true story, about the subject

Word Origins

Where do English words come from? Did someone wake up one morning and decide to call that thing that takes your temperature a thermometer? No. Most English words come from other languages, such as Greek, Latin, German, and French, to name a few.

Thermometer comes from the Greek words *thermo*, meaning "heat," and *meter*, meaning "an instrument that measures something." Other words with *thermo* in them also have to do with heat, such as *thermos*. A thermos is a container that keeps liquids hot. Other words with *meter* at the end have to do with measuring something, such as *pedometer*. A pedometer measures how far a person walks.

Identify Main Idea and Supporting Details

Before an author writes a biography, he or she creates an outline of information. Each section of the outline discusses a portion, or "big idea," of the person's life. Each section contains specific details supporting each big idea. After the outline is complete, the author incorporates the big ideas and supporting details into one biography. These big ideas are called main ideas. Main ideas often appear in the first sentence of a paragraph. These main ideas are called stated main ideas. Other times main ideas are unstated, or implied. Readers must use what they read to figure out the main idea.

The World and Lives of Caesar and Cleopatra

Today, Italy, Greece, and Egypt are independent countries. But a few thousand years ago, the governments and people of each place were interconnected. Italy as we know it today didn't exist. Instead, it was the center of the powerful ancient Roman Republic. The Republic expanded and spread as its army conquered territory after territory. Julius Caesar was one of three leaders of the Republic in 60 B.C.E.

At the time, Caesar and the Romans sought control of Egypt, whose rulers were descendants of ancient Greece. The Greeks, under the leadership of Alexander the Great, had freed Egypt from Persian rule in 332 B.C.E. Ptolemy (TAH-leh-mee), a former general in Alexander's army, founded Egypt's next ruling dynasty in 305 B.C.E. Cleopatra would be the last in the line of rulers descended from Ptolemy.

When Cleopatra was born, the once-glorious Egyptian Empire was in a state of decline. The Ptolemies had turned out to be weak rulers. By the time Caesar and Cleopatra met, Egypt's treasury had become severely depleted. Egypt was still an independent country, but it had grown increasingly dependent on Rome for economic help and military protection. Under her rule, Cleopatra restored much of Egypt's wealth. Julius Caesar's grandnephew would turn Egypt into a province of ancient Rome.

Julius Caesar

100 B.C.E.–44 B.C.E.

100 B.C.E.
Gaius Julius Caesar is born in Rome.

75
Caesar is captured by pirates; after he is released, he returns and executes them.

69
Cleopatra is born.

63
Octavian, Caesar's grandnephew (who later is known as Augustus Caesar), is born.

60
Caesar is elected consul and forms First Triumvirate with Pompey and Crassus.

47
Caesar defeats Ptolemy and reinstalls Cleopatra and her brother Ptolemy XIV onto the throne. Later this year, Cleopatra and Caesar's son, Caesarion (Ptolemy XV), is born.

45
Caesar adopts Octavian as his heir.

44
Caesar is murdered by Brutus and Cassius in the Roman Senate, March 15.

43
Antony, Octavian, and Lepidus form the Second Triumvirate.

42
Antony and Octavian defeat Brutus and Cassius, Caesar's main assassins, in the battle of Philippi (in Greece). Brutus and Cassius both commit suicide.

Cleopatra

69 B.C.E.–30 B.C.E.

53
Crassus, part of the First Triumvirate, is killed in Parthia. With Crassus dead, a power struggle begins between Caesar and Pompey, the two remaining triumvirs.

51
Cleopatra's father, Auletes, dies, leaving his throne to 18-year-old Cleopatra and her younger brother, Ptolemy XIII, to rule together.

49
Ptolemy drives Cleopatra out of Egypt. She flees to Syria. Roman civil war erupts. Caesar crosses the Rubicon to fight Pompey.

48
Caesar defeats Pompey at the battle of Pharsalus. Pompey is murdered in Egypt. Caesar is now the most powerful ruler in the world.

48
Caesar and Cleopatra meet and form an alliance. Caesar backs her in a civil war against her brother.

41
Antony and Cleopatra form an alliance.

34
Antony grants several Eastern territories to Cleopatra and her children, which outrages many Romans.

33
Octavian declares war on Cleopatra.

31
Antony and Cleopatra are defeated by Octavian at the battle of Actium (western Greece). The two flee to Alexandria.

30
Antony commits suicide. Cleopatra commits suicide. Octavian has Caesarion (son of Cleopatra and Caesar) killed. Octavian makes Egypt a Roman province.

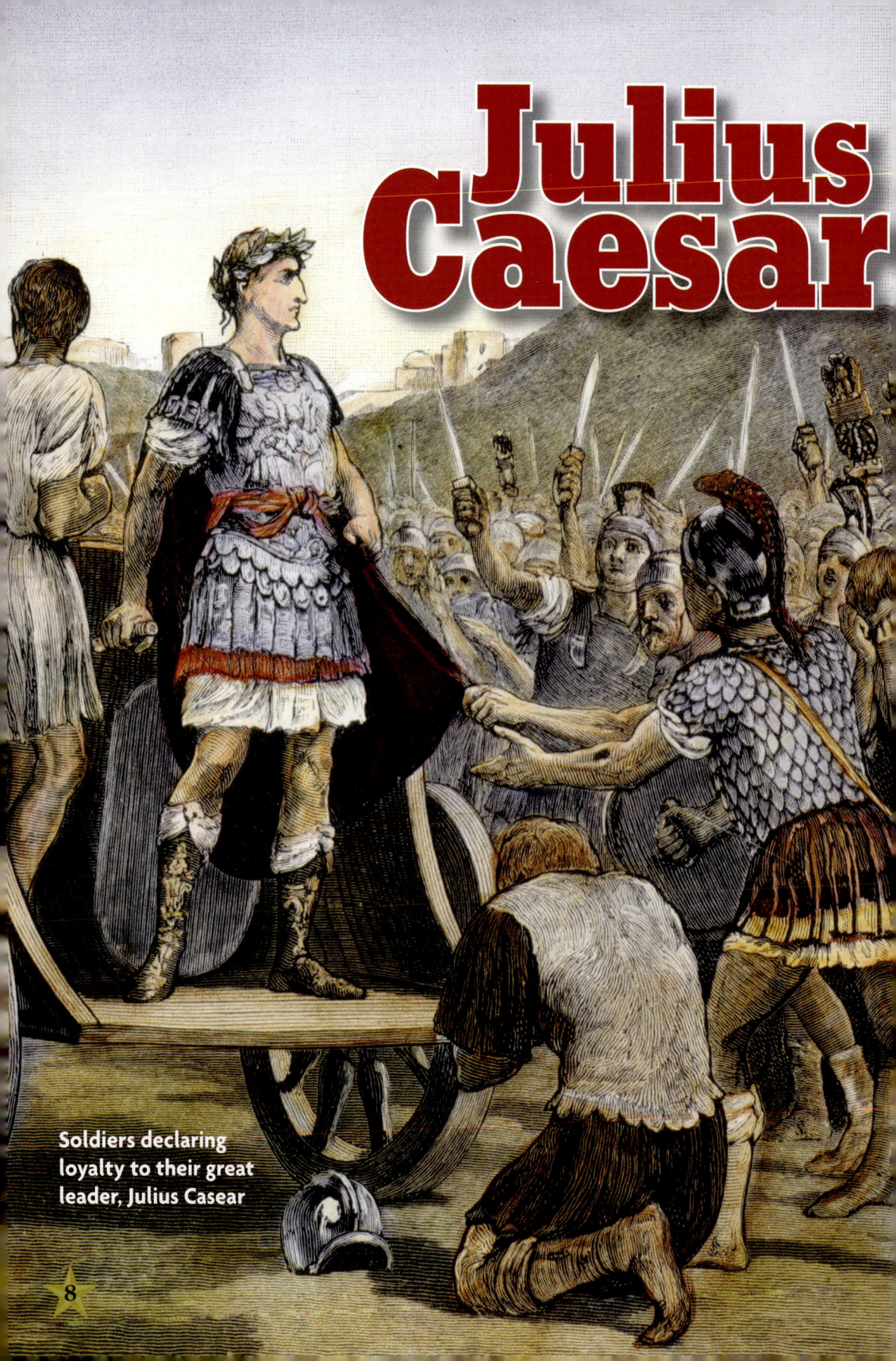

Julius Caesar

Soldiers declaring loyalty to their great leader, Julius Casear

What sort of man was Julius Caesar? By all accounts he was highly intelligent, a brilliant military tactician, and a skillful orator. He was handsome, although he worried about his thinning hair. Humble he most certainly was not.

By the time he reached the age of about 50, Caesar had transformed himself from a vain, unscrupulous spendthrift into a brilliant general, an elegant orator and writer, and a profound and conscientious leader.

Having transformed himself, Julius Caesar transformed Rome—from a small, if powerful, republic mired in corruption and violence into a vast domain on the verge of becoming one of the greatest empires the world has ever known.

Fifteen centuries after Caesar's death, Shakespeare wrote a play about him. And today, twenty centuries later, we remember Caesar as one of the greatest statesmen in history.

His Early Years

In 100 B.C.E., Gaius Julius Caesar was born into a noble but impoverished family. Historians are not certain whether or not Caesar's mother, Aurelia, gave birth to him by Caesarean section, the operation that bears his name.

Like all nobly born Roman boys, Caesar grew up trained for a life in politics, studying both Greek and Latin literature, **philosophy**, and **rhetoric**.

At 17, Caesar married a woman named Cornelia. Two years later they had a daughter named Julia.

Julius Caesar

As a young man, Caesar served as a military aide to a Roman general in Asia. He won the admiration of the soldiers because of his willingness to endure the same living conditions that they did.

In 75 B.C.E., pirates seized Caesar's ship as it sailed toward what is now Turkey. The pirates quickly realized that Caesar must be a wealthy man, so they took him hostage and demanded a huge ransom for his release.

Caesar scoffed at his captors. He told them he was worth much more than the ransom they were demanding and suggested they ask for more than double that amount. Bewildered, the pirates did as he suggested. Caesar sent his servants off to collect the money from his friends.

As soon as Caesar's friends had raised the ransom and won his release, he headed for a nearby port, hired several ships full of men, and chased down his former captors. He promptly had the pirates executed.

An Ambitious Man

Caesar's wife Cornelia died in 69 B.C.E. A year later, Caesar married Pompeia. She was the wealthy granddaughter of Sulla, who had been an important leader in Roman politics. In ancient Rome, members of the middle and upper classes often married for political reasons, or to bolster a family's wealth or social status, rather than for love.

The politically ambitious Caesar made many allies as well as many enemies. One of the people he supported was Crassus, the richest man in Rome. In return, Crassus lent Caesar huge amounts of money.

When Caesar was about 35, he was elected commissioner of public works. He probably bribed many voters in order to get elected, using Crassus's money.

In ancient Rome, slaves—many of whom had been captured in battles—made up as much as a third of the population.

Because slaves performed nearly all of the manual labor in Rome, the poorer classes of "freemen"—known as the **plebeians**—enjoyed a great deal of leisure time. As commissioner, Caesar spent huge sums of money to entertain the plebeians with amusements and games, including chariot races and **gladiator** contests.

In 63 B.C.E., Caesar beat out two prominent opponents to win the title of chief priest. A year after that he became a *praetor*, or judge. Later that year, he divorced Pompeia when she was accused of having an affair with another man.

In 60 B.C.E., Caesar formed a three-way alliance, called a **triumvirate**, with two other men. One of the men was the wealthy Crassus. The other was named Pompey, a respected general. To cement the alliance, Pompey married Caesar's daughter, Julia. (She would later die in childbirth.) Caesar in turn married Calpurnia, who was the daughter of one of Pompey's close associates.

Caesar, ambitious as ever, knew he lacked real military experience. So he arranged to have himself appointed governor of a group of **provinces** just outside of Rome, most notably a region known as Gaul, which today is part of France.

Watching a gladiator pitted against a lion was considered entertainment in ancient Rome.

The Conquests in Gaul

In the year 58 B.C.E., Caesar traveled to Gaul to conquer the roaming tribes of people the Romans considered to be barbarians. The wars in Gaul dragged on for several years. While the fighting wore on, Caesar wrote a book he called *The Wars in Gaul*, in which he recorded the events of his campaign.

In 52 B.C.E., a chieftain from Gaul united nearly all the Gallic tribes against Caesar. He very nearly succeeded in beating Caesar's armies. But Caesar outmaneuvered his opponent with brilliant tactical planning and forced him to surrender. The Gallic chieftain was led in chains back to Rome.

Gaul now became a province of the Roman Empire. This victory was momentous both for Caesar and for Rome. By conquering Gaul, Caesar succeeded in protecting Rome from foreign invasions for several hundred more years. He also added over 200,000 square miles to Rome's dominions.

Caesar leading his army across the Rubicon

Caesar and Cleopatra

Meanwhile, Crassus, one of the triumvirs, was killed in 53 B.C.E. while battling the Parthians in Syria. His death left Pompey and Caesar in charge. The two had never gotten along. Now, each man clearly wanted to be the sole ruler of Rome. With Caesar far away in Gaul, Pompey seized power. He convinced the Senate—Rome's political body of 100 leaders—to demand that Caesar resign.

Far away from Rome, Caesar knew he had a decision to make. Although he was aware that he had many enemies in Rome, he also felt confident that his soldiers loved him. He had shared their hardships and perils—and had doubled their pay!

Caesar fully understood that he was breaking Roman law by moving troops across the border of his province and into Italy. Nevertheless, he led his troops across the Rubicon, a small river that marked the boundary between Gaul and Italy. (Nowadays the expression *to cross the Rubicon* means to do something from which there is no turning back.)

Pompey

In the civil war that followed, Caesar proved himself a superior military commander, and Pompey surrendered. Caesar pardoned Pompey's chief generals, Brutus and Cassius.

Meanwhile, Pompey fled to Egypt, hoping to find protection there. But he arrived in Alexandria when it was in the midst of a power struggle for the throne between Cleopatra and her brother Ptolemy XIII. Pompey was murdered by Ptolemy's associates.

Caesar came to Egypt a few days later, furious about Pompey's assassination, but also to demand repayment for money Cleopatra's father had borrowed from Rome. He sent for Cleopatra, believing she might become an ally of his, and the two fell in love with one another. (Read Cleopatra's biography on pages 18–27 for details.)

Julius Caesar

Caesar remained with Cleopatra in Egypt for almost a year, during which time he restored her to the Egyptian throne and fathered a child with her, Ptolemy XV, whose given name was Caesarion.

After leaving Egypt, Caesar fought a battle in southern Asia and sent a letter back to Rome describing his exploits. His words "*Veni, vidi, vici*" ("I came, I saw, I conquered") are famous to this day.

Caesar the Great Statesman

Back in Rome, in the summer of 47 B.C.E., Caesar embraced his role as the most powerful man in the world. He ordered statuses of himself to be carved. He had his face imprinted on Roman coins. But he also enacted many important new laws. He reduced taxes for the poor. He began great building projects. He protected the Jews and allowed them to practice their religion freely. He lengthened the calendar to 365 ¼ days. One writer from Caesar's time, Cicero, who disliked Caesar, grumbled that Caesar was "not content to rule the world but must rule the stars!"

Caesar's emperor-like behavior concerned many Roman senators, some of whom feared losing their power if Caesar became king. Others worried about his relationship with Cleopatra, who had come to live in Rome as Caesar's guest. What if Caesar married her and moved the capital to Alexandria?

People began plotting Caesar's death and chose March 15 as the date he would be killed. Many senators were involved in the

Brutus, one of Julius Caesar's assassins, may have been his son.

plot, but the leaders were Brutus and Cassius, the two generals whom Caesar had pardoned.

To complicate matters further, it is widely believed that Brutus was Caesar's own son. Caesar had had an affair with Brutus's mother that coincided with Brutus's birth. Whether or not Brutus was his son, Caesar was extremely fond of the young man.

The Ides of March

According to some ancient historians, a soothsayer warned Caesar to "Beware the ides of March," which March 15 was known as. Caesar's wife and friends feared for his safety and urged him not to go to the Senate meeting.

But he did go. As he entered the doorway, a group of men attacked him with knives. He tried to ward off their blows, but when he saw that one of his would-be assassins was Brutus, he cried, "You too, my child?" and ended his resistance. He died of 23 stab wounds.

Caesar's death was a major tragedy of history. He had become one of the greatest statesmen who would ever live. Painters, writers, poets and sculptors would celebrate his life for centuries to come.

This nineteenth-century painting shows the assassination of Julius Caesar in the Roman Senate.

Reread the Biography

Analyze the Subject
- When and where was Julius Caesar born?
- What were some of Julius Caesar's accomplishments?
- What kind of challenges did Julius Caesar face?
- Julius Caesar was a very confident person. Identify two examples of this.
- How did Julius Caesar's life end?
- Julius Caesar's life has carried over into today's culture. Identify two examples of this.
- Would you want the power that Julius Caesar had? Why or why not?

Focus on Comprehension: Identify Main Idea and Supporting Details
- Reread "An Ambitious Man." What is the main idea of this section? What details support the main idea?
- Reread "Caesar the Great Statesman." What is the stated main idea of this section?
- The last section is about Caesar's death. What details support this main idea?

Analyze the Tools Writers Use: Strong Lead
- Reread the lead for this biography. What type of lead did the author use? Direct or indirect? How can you tell?
- Did the lead "hook" you as a reader? If so, why?
- What did you expect to learn after reading the lead?
- In what other ways could this lead have been written?

Focus on Words: Word Origins

Make a chart like the one below. Use a dictionary or the Internet to identify each word's origin and its history, such as when it was first used and by whom. Finally, write a definition for the word.

Page	Word	Word Origins	Word History	Definition
9	philosophy			
9	rhetoric			
11	plebeians			
11	gladiator			
11	triumvirate			
11	provinces			

gladiator battle at the Coliseum

Cleopatra

This wood engraving from the nineteenth century shows Cleopatra during the Battle of Actium in 31 B.C.E.

What is it about Cleopatra, the last queen of Egypt, that has fascinated writers and artists for centuries?

It's difficult to confirm the facts of Cleopatra's life. So much about her is unknown or has been slanted by later writers. After her death, the Romans intentionally destroyed many of the documents of her reign. Later accounts of Cleopatra's life were written by Greek and Roman writers, who either vilified her as an evil temptress, or embellished descriptions of her beauty, talents, and accomplishments. The lines blur between fact and myth.

What is certain is that Cleopatra was highly intelligent and courageous, a wise **administrator**, and fiercely loyal to the two men she loved, one for whom she sacrificed her life.

The Struggle for the Throne

Cleopatra was born in Alexandria, Egypt, in 69 B.C.E. Not much is known about her early years. Many people are surprised to learn that she was Greek, a descendant of the Macedonian general Ptolemy. She may have had light-colored hair and, judging from her images on coins and statues, was certainly striking in appearance if not beautiful. She spoke many languages, including Greek, Egyptian, and Syrian. The fact that she spoke Egyptian, the language of her subjects, set her apart from the other Ptolemies, none of whom deigned to learn the language of the people over whom they ruled.

> The author hooks the reader by asking a provocative question about the subject of the biography.

> The author provides details about Cleopatra's personality that made her intriguing.

> The author provides the place and date of birth of her subject. She also establishes that, from a very young age, Cleopatra was impressive looking and well-educated.

Cleopatra

> The author describes two important events that took place in Cleopatra's life when she was a young woman: fleeing Egypt and meeting Caesar.

When Cleopatra was 18, her father, Ptolemy XI, died, leaving her and her 10-year-old brother to rule together. They were supposed to marry one another, according to Egyptian custom. But they did not get along. Young Ptolemy XIII's advisers drove Cleopatra out of Egypt and probably planned to have her killed.

Meanwhile, one of the Roman triumvirs, Pompey, was murdered in Egypt in 48 B.C.E. Four days later, Julius Caesar arrived in Egypt. Caesar learned from his barber that Cleopatra's brother and his advisers were planning to kill him. So he sent for Cleopatra, probably with the intention of forming an alliance with her. In a characteristically bold move, Cleopatra had herself rolled into a carpet and was brought to Caesar's room in secret. She was 21. Caesar was 52.

Did they fall in love immediately? No one knows for certain. Her intelligence and beauty seem to have charmed Caesar. What did she see in this much-older man? Cleopatra was a practical person. She needed help opposing her brother, and it was handy to partner with the most powerful man in the Western world. Still, it seems evident that their admiration quickly became mutual.

Caesar promptly backed Cleopatra against her brother. He had Ptolemy's advisers assassinated. Then he sent for reinforcements, and the Roman army vanquished the Egyptians who had been plotting to kill Caesar. Ptolemy was drowned as he tried to flee from the Roman troops.

Cleopatra married her surviving brother, 12-year-old Ptolemy XIV, and ascended the throne. She was now the reigning queen of Egypt.

Life After Caesar

Caesar returned to Rome in 47 B.C.E. bringing with him Cleopatra and their young son, Caesarion, as his official guests. Many Romans were appalled that the Egyptian queen had come to Rome to be near the married Caesar.

A few years later, after Caesar was murdered, Cleopatra fled back to Egypt.

This oil painting from 1637 is called *Caesar Leads Cleopatra Back to the Throne of Egypt.*

Cleopatra

About a year after Caesar's death, three powerful Romans formed a second triumvirate. One was Caesar's 18-year-old adopted son, his grandnephew Octavian. (Caesar had left no legitimate male heirs.) The second was a general named Marcus Lepidus. The third was one of Caesar's most trusted military generals, a man named Marcus Antonius (or Mark Antony, or just Antony). Meanwhile, Caesar's two main assassins, Brutus and Cassius, began raising troops in Greece to fight the new triumvirs.

The author describes how Cleopatra's personality and intelligence had a positive effect on the Egyptian economy.

By now Egypt's treasury had recovered from the misrule of Cleopatra's father. Thanks to Cleopatra's expansion of **agriculture** and sound administrative decisions regarding exports to other countries of grain, linen, and oil, Egypt had grown wealthy again.

Cleopatra was forced to choose sides in the Roman conflict. Should she support the power-hungry triumvirs or the men who had murdered Caesar? Cleopatra, fiercely loyal to her dead lover, sided with the triumvirs. In 42 B.C.E., Brutus and Cassius went to war against Antony and Octavian in northern Greece. Brutus and Cassius were defeated, and both committed suicide. Thus ended the Roman Republic.

The author shows how the subject's actions influenced history.

Mark Antony

Cleopatra, Antony, and Octavian

The three triumvirs divided the Roman empire among themselves, assigning each a portion over which to rule.

Antony was granted power over Greece, Asia Minor, and Cleopatra's Egypt. He hoped to conquer Parthia for Rome, but he knew he needed vast sums of money to wage the campaign—and Cleopatra was rich. So in the summer of 41 B.C.E., he summoned Cleopatra, who was now about 28 years old, to his headquarters in Tarsus (in southern Asia Minor).

According to a Greek writer and historian named Plutarch, Cleopatra made a memorable entrance. She sailed up the river in a barge with a golden stern and heavily perfumed purple sails. Her rowers, beautiful handmaidens to the queen, dipped their silver oars in time to the music of a flute. People came running from all directions to watch.

The author could not interview the subject of this biography, but she includes information from a Greek writer who lived around the time of Cleopatra.

This fresco painting of Antony and Cleopatra is by Giovanni Tiepolo, a famous Italian artist of the 1700s.

Cleopatra

Whether or not this story is true, Cleopatra had proven to be a master at creating a dramatic public image of herself. She shrewdly relied on visual **spectacle**, as few of the people in her kingdom knew how to read and write. Antony appears to have been instantly smitten with her.

The queen made an agreement with Antony. In exchange for his protection against her enemies, she promised to provide him with money to fund his military campaign.

> Whatever her initial motives for forming an alliance with Antony, Cleopatra soon fell in love with him. Forgetting that he had an empire to rule, Antony remained in Alexandria with Cleopatra over the winter. She became pregnant with his child.

The author has dedicated sections of the biography to Mark Antony, a major influence in Cleopatra's life.

In 40 B.C.E., Antony left Cleopatra to travel back to Rome. While he had been gone, his wife, Fulvia, and brother, Lucius, had led a failed rebellion against Octavian.

Antony repaired his relations with Octavian. Soon after that, Fulvia died. Antony married Octavian's sister, Octavia, in order to cement the bond between the two triumvirs. A few weeks after Antony's marriage, Cleopatra gave birth to twins—Antony was the father.

> With Antony in Rome, the ever-practical Cleopatra spent the next several years concentrating on ruling her kingdom and increasing the Egyptian treasury. In so doing, she became one of the richest and most powerful women in the world.

The author includes information that gives readers insight into why the subject is worthy of a biography.

In 37 B.C.E., Antony left for Syria, intent on waging war against Parthia. He soon sent for Cleopatra. His campaign against the Parthians failed, but he remained with Cleopatra, leaving his sad wife, Octavia, back in Rome.

In 35 B.C.E., Cleopatra gave birth to her third child by Antony. Antony established Cleopatra and her son Caesarion as joint rulers of Egypt and Cyprus. He also bestowed titles and lands in the eastern provinces on the children he had fathered with Cleopatra. Many Romans were shocked by his behavior.

Back in Rome, Octavian removed Lepidus from power and had him arrested. Octavian then set about stirring up Roman anger against Antony. He denounced Antony's abandonment of Octavia. He convinced the Senate that Cleopatra had bewitched Antony and was scheming to take over the empire.

In 32 B.C.E., the shrewd Octavian declared war—not against the popular Antony, but against Cleopatra. Privately, he knew that by waging war against Cleopatra, he was waging war against Antony. If Octavian defeated Antony, he would become the sole ruler of the new Roman Empire.

Octavian

Last Days Together

Antony and Cleopatra raised a huge army to fight Octavian. They recruited soldiers from the eastern provinces, many of whom hoped to gain independence from Rome.

In 30 B.C.E., an immense battle took place at Actium, in western Greece. Octavian's troops prevailed. Antony and Cleopatra fled to Alexandria. They knew that all was now lost.

Octavian sent a message to Cleopatra. He told her that if she agreed to kill Antony, her own life would be spared. Octavian underestimated Cleopatra's love and loyalty. She refused.

Meanwhile, Antony received a message that Cleopatra was dead. Having lost the battle with Octavian, and believing his beloved to be dead, he must have despaired of having anything more to live for. According to Plutarch's version of the story, Antony stabbed himself with his sword. Servants carried the **mortally** wounded man to Cleopatra. He died in her arms.

Readers learn the extent of Cleopatra's feelings for Antony. Biographies are not just facts and accomplishments.

This wood engraving from the nineteenth century features the defeat of Antony and Cleopatra at Actium.

Tragic End

Cleopatra was now 39 years old, and though still living in her palace, she was a virtual prisoner of Octavian. Octavian, who clearly respected her, seemed to have no intention of executing her. But she was convinced she would be taken to Rome and paraded before the people as a conquered queen. To spare herself such humiliation, she dressed herself in royal robes and poisoned herself with the bite of a deadly asp, a type of snake. Her handmaidens did the same.

Octavian honored Cleopatra's wish to be buried next to Antony. But to avoid any future power struggles, he ordered the child she had borne with Caesar, Caesarion, to be slain.

In a purely noble act, Antony's sad and neglected wife, Octavia, took in Antony and Cleopatra's children and raised them as her own.

Octavian became known as Augustus Caesar, the first leader of the Roman Empire. Egypt's long history as an independent nation came to an end.

But Cleopatra's story—her incredible life, her capacity for love and loyalty, her tragic death, and her unparalleled mystique—lives on to this day.

The author recounts the sad aftermath to Cleopatra's death, but she leaves readers wanting to know more about the subject.

This 1769 oil painting shows Octavian at Cleopatra's deathbed.

Reread the Biography

Analyze the Subject
- When and where was Cleopatra born?
- What were some of Cleopatra's accomplishments?
- What kind of challenges did Cleopatra face?
- Many people were involved in Cleopatra's life. Identify three and explain their involvement in her life.
- Under what conditions did Cleopatra's life end?
- Would you want to have Cleopatra's power? Why or why not?

Focus on Comprehension: Identify Main Idea and Supporting Details
- "Life After Caesar" is about some of the things Cleopatra did after Caesar was murdered. What details support this main idea?
- Identify two stated main ideas in this biography.
- The last section is about Cleopatra's last days. What details support this main idea?

Focus on Including Questions
Many authors include questions in biographies because they make readers stop and think while they are reading. Identify places in the text where the author included questions. What do those questions make you think about? How do they help you understand the biography?

Analyze the Tools Writers Use: Strong Lead

- Reread the lead for this biography. What type of lead did the author use? Direct or indirect? How can you tell?
- Did the lead "hook" you as a reader? Why?
- What did you expect to learn after reading the lead?
- In what other ways could this lead have been written?

Focus on Words: Word Origins

Make a chart like the one below. Use a dictionary or the Internet to identify each word's origin and its history, such as when it was first used and by whom. Finally, write a definition for the word.

Page	Word	Word Origins	Word History	Definition
19	administrator			
22	agriculture			
24	spectacle			
26	mortally			

Cleopatra greets Julius Caesar.

The Writer's Craft

How does an author write a BIOGRAPHY?

Reread "Cleopatra" and think about what the author did to write this biography. How did she describe Cleopatra's life? How did she show what Cleopatra accomplished?

1. Decide on Someone to Write About

Remember: A biography is a factual retelling of someone's life. Therefore, you must research his or her life and, if possible, interview the person. In "Cleopatra," the author wants to show readers that Cleopatra was an exceptionally intelligent, strategic, and strong woman and ruler, especially given the complicated, warlike, male-dominated time in which she lived.

2. Decide Who Else Needs to Be in the Biography

Other people will likely be an important part of your subject's life. Ask yourself:

- Who was in the person's family?
- Who were the person's friends and neighbors?
- Who did the person go to school with or work with?
- Who helped or hurt the person?
- Which people should I include?
- How will I describe these people?

Person or Group	How They Impacted Cleopatra's Life
Ptolemy XIII's advisers	caused Cleopatra's brother to turn against his sister and co-ruler of Egypt and force her to flee for her life to Syria
Julius Caesar	restored Cleopatra to the throne and became the father of her first son
Mark Antony	was her last great love; she killed herself after he died in her arms

Many paintings and engravings of the beautiful Cleopatra have been created over the centuries.

Recall Events and Setting

Jot down notes about what happened in the subject's life and where these things happened. Ask yourself:

- Where did the person's experiences take place? How will I describe these places?
- What were the most important events in his or her life?
- What situations or problems did the person experience?
- What did the person accomplish?
- What questions might my readers have about the subject that I could answer in my biography?

Subject	Setting(s)	Important Events
Cleopatra	Egypt, Rome, Tarsus	1. escapes to Syria at 18 when her brother and co-ruler threatens her life
		2. is restored to the throne by Julius Caesar
		3. falls in love with Caesar and has his son
		4. travels to Rome with her son and Caesar
		5. returns to Egypt after Caesar is assassinated
		6. meets and forms an alliance with Mark Antony and falls in love with him
		7. Octavian declares war on her.
		8. Antony dies in her arms.
		9. in despair, kills herself with the fatal bite of an asp

Glossary

administrator (ad-MIH-nih-stray-ter) a person in charge of government or business affairs (page 19)

agriculture (A-grih-kul-cher) an organized system of farming (page 22)

gladiator (GLA-dee-ay-ter) a man in ancient Rome who entertained an audience by fighting against a gladiator or a wild animal to the death (page 11)

mortally (MOR-tuh-lee) fatally; to death (page 26)

philosophy (fih-LA-suh-fee) study of ideas and values, based on logic (page 9)

plebeians (plih-BEE-un) lower-class Roman citizens (page 11)

provinces (PRAH-vins) countries or regions (often ruled by another power) (page 11)

rhetoric (REH-tuh-rik) the art of speaking or writing effectively (page 9)

spectacle (SPEK-tih-kul) unusual, eye-catching, event (page 24)

triumvirate (try-UM-vuh-rit) a ruling body of three (page 11)